Kipper had spots.

1

Biff and Chip had spots, too.

The doctor came.

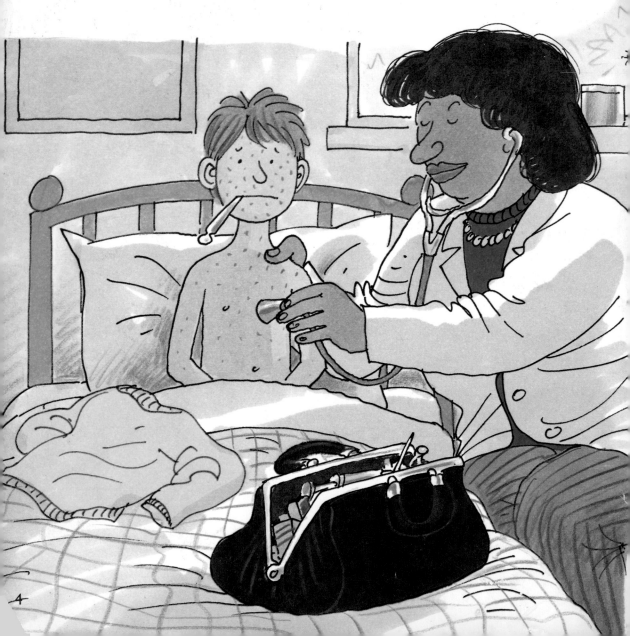

'Stay in bed,' she said.

Mum had spots.

'Stay in bed, too,' said the doctor.

Dad looked after everyone.

He put the washing out.

He went shopping.

'What a job!' said Dad.

Everyone got better.

14

'Oh no!' said Mum.

Dad had spots.